SOME PARTS are NOT for SHARING

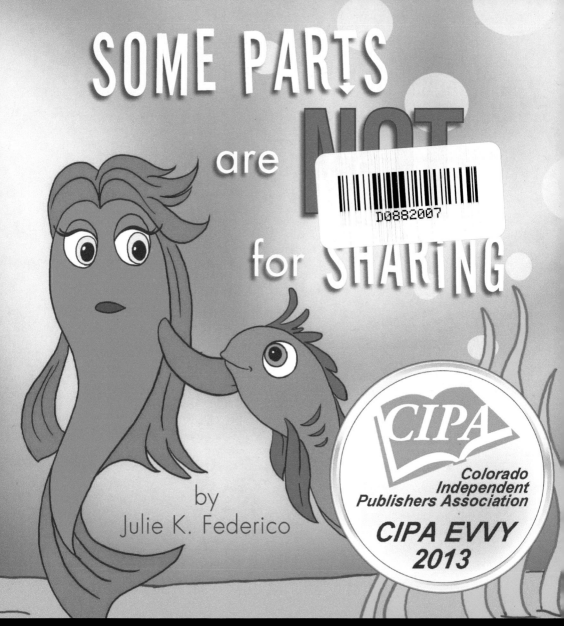

by
Julie K. Federico

Published by Ingram Spark

1246 Heil Quaker Blvd
La Vergne, TN 37086

Call (855) 997-7275
ingramsparksupport@ingramcontent.com

United Kingdom: ingramsparkinternational@ingramcontent.com
Australia: IngramSparkAustralia@ingramcontent.com
http://www.ingramspark.com

Book design copyright © 2018 by Ingram Spark. All rights reserved.
Cover design & Interior design by Eddie Russell
Illustration by Kurt Jones
Conceptual reference by Sarah Page and Amanda Green

Published in the United States of America

ISBN: 978-1-60696-603-7
1. Abuse Education: 6 months and up
2. Pre school/kindergarten
08.09.24

DEDICATION

This book is dedicated to Amelia, Olivia,
and children everywhere.

ACKNOWLEDGEMENT

I would like to thank God for giving me the words
for this book, and for the opportunity to publish
it.   I am quietly ending childhood sexual abuse
one book at a time.

INTRODUCTION

Each day, four children in the United States die from some form of abuse. One out of every four girls and one out of every six boys will have been sexually molested by the time they reach the age of eighteen. Most of this abuse begins before the child is four years old. We need to take every precaution for protecting our children from this heinous problem!

This book is ideal as an introduction to basic body safety rules for the very young child, allowing parents to begin educating their child long before the age of four. "Say no and get away. Tell a trusted adult." These are the crucial concepts to offer to the very young child. It is the adult's responsibility to provide early learning for protecting their child and this short story will assist them with the process.

Marilyn Carson
Prevention Education Specialist
ChildHelp

Everyone has a body.
Even fish have bodies.

Some parts of our bodies we share with others.

For example our hands when we high five someone

or shake their hand.

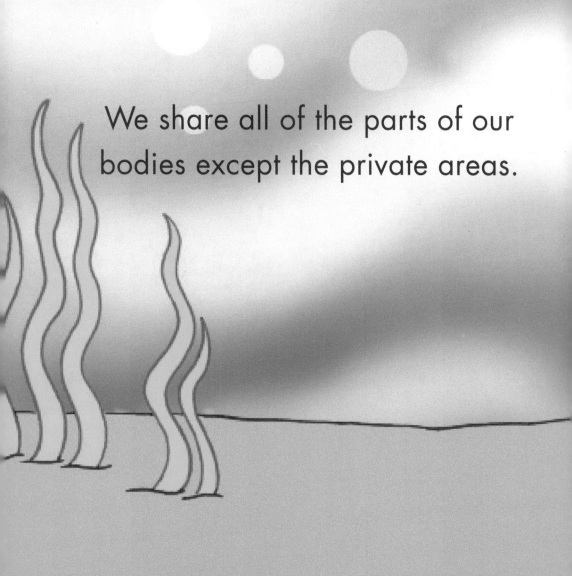

We share all of the parts of our bodies except the private areas.

The private areas are any area a swimsuit covers.

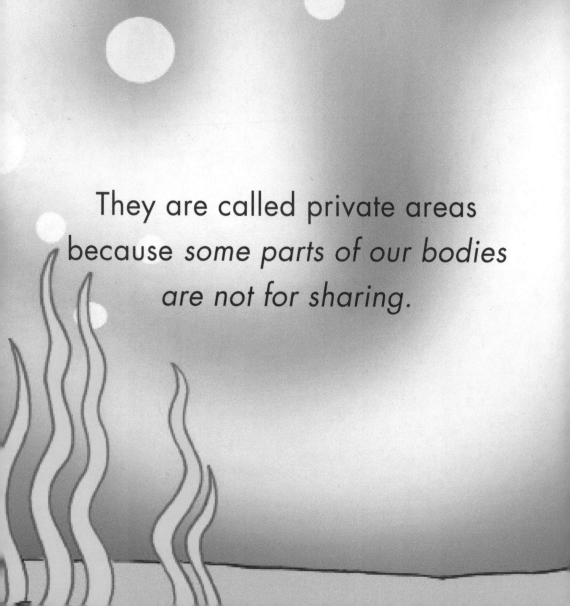

They are called private areas
because *some parts of our bodies
are not for sharing.*

If someone asks to touch or touches the private areas say, "No!" and run to find a trusted adult.

There are some parts of our bodies
we share with others, but some parts
are not for sharing.

THE END

Some Parts are NOT for Sharing Study Guide

Objective:
Students will understand what body safety is and how to protect their bodies. Students will learn who they should tell if someone is touching them in an unsafe way.

Discussion Questions:

Before today has anyone in the group had training on body safety? What you think body safety is?

After reading Some Parts are NOT for Sharing we learned what parts of our bodies we share with others. What are the parts of our bodies that we share with others? What are the parts we do not share?

What should someone do if they encounter unwanted touch? Who should they tell?   What should the student do if the person they tell does not listen to them?

Mention mandatory reporters. All school personnel are mandatory reporters students need to know that they can self disclose to anyone at the school about unwanted touch.

It is helpful for students to know that if they need to talk to their teacher about this they should say, "Mrs. _____ I need to talk to you about the fish book." Teachers are the busiest people in the world. They need this alert to be sure to follow up with the student and not to let this go unattended.

Optional worksheet for students:

1. What was your favorite part of the book Some Parts are NOT for Sharing?

2. Have you ever-experienced unwanted touch? Circle one.

Yes   No

3. If you answered Yes to question #2 would you like to talk about this? Circle one.

Yes   No

4. Do you have a trusted adult in your life? Circle one.

Yes   NO

5. Do you have any other questions about this lesson?

CPSIA information can be obtained
at www.ICGtesting.com
Printed in the USA
LVHW071622300323
742951LV00012B/80

* 9 7 8 1 6 0 6 9 6 6 0 3 7 *